Dogs Bring Newspapers
But Cats Bring Mice
AND OTHER FASCINATING FACTS ABOUT ANIMAL BEHAVIOR

by Melvin and Gilda Berger

SCHOLASTIC INC.
New York   Toronto   London   Auckland   Sydney
Mexico City   New Delhi   Hong Kong   Buenos Aires

For dear Max, who loves animals

ISBN 0-439-66433-0

12 11 10 9 8 7 6 5 4 3 2   4 5 6 7 8 9/0

Printed in the U.S.A.
First printing, September 2004
Interior art by Rémy Simard
Design by Janet Kusmierski, *Dedicated to Sparky, 1996-2004*
Photo research by Sarah Longacre

cm = centimeter

g = gram

kg = kilogram

km = kilometer

kph = kilometers per hour

l = liter

m = meter

t = metric ton

INTRODUCTION

Why does a cat rub its head against you? How does a dog show it wants to play? *Dogs Bring Newspapers But Cats Bring Mice* takes a close-up look at some animals' curious behaviors. Read on!

There are more than one million different kinds, or species, of animals on earth. Each species has its own size, color, and shape. And each differs from the rest in what it does and how it responds to its surroundings. The way an animal acts is known as its *behavior*.

The most important kinds of behavior are inborn, or built-in. Animals do many things without having to learn what to do or how to do it. Bats sleep upside down. Cats crouch down to eat. Horses point their ears in the direction of sounds.

Other kinds of behavior are learned. Wolf mothers teach their cubs to hunt. Chimpanzees learn to communicate with people by sign language. Elephants can obey dozens of voice commands.

Animals behave in strange and wonderful ways. In this book, you'll discover how certain animals' behavior helps them—and sometimes helps us—to survive.

ANIMALS ON THE GROUND
CATS

Clever Hunters

The house cat is a close cousin of the lion, tiger, leopard, panther, and jaguar. But did you know that the house cat also behaves like the bigger members of i_____

Big and small cats a_____ nals, or prey, for food. Cats snec_____ Or a cat lies waiting for its victim_____ Cats use their very sharp claws a_____ er senses of sight, smell, and hear_____ ellent memory allows them to_____ hey once had good hunting.

Speedy Fact 1
A cat lashes its tail when angry and gently twitches it back and forth when contented.

Cats eat fast.
This prevents other animals from stealing their dinner.

Speedy Fact 3
Cats use their whiskers to feel things move—even in total darkness.

Speedy Fact 4
Cats may hiss or spit, usually at other cats or dogs, to warn them to stay away.

Speedy Fact 5
Cats arch their backs when frightened. Their fur stands on end and their tails puff up so they look larger and fiercer than they really are.

Speedy Fact
1

Cats never purr when they're alone.

Cats and People

Cats and humans have lived together since ancient times. The Egyptians worshipped cats as gods.

Many cat owners believe that cats can be tamed. But cats rarely change their basic behavior. A cat playing with a toy behaves as if the toy were a mouse the cat had caught.

Cats may live in a house with no real enemies and plenty of food. Yet, the cats will still catch mice and bring them home. Mother house cats will still seek a safe, dark place to have their young. And, as their kittens grow up among people, the mother cats will still teach their young how to avoid danger and how to hunt for food.

Speedy Fact
2

Most cats "meow" to attract attention or to get someone to feed them.

Speedy Fact
3

A cat rubs its head against you as a greeting. This leaves the cat's scent, which says, "You're mine."

HOW CATS COMMUNICATE WITH SOUND	
Sound	**Meaning**
Purr	Happy
Low meow	Upset
High meow	Excited
Hiss or growl	Scared or angry
Chirp	Sees prey
Yowl	Wants something
Scream	In pain
Screech	Hostile

LIONS
Living in Prides

Lions are the only members of the cat family that live in groups. A group of lions is called a *pride*. A pride can have as many as 35 members, including many females (lionesses), young lions (cubs), and one or two males (lions).

Male lions defend their pride's territory by roaring loudly and marking trees and bushes with their urine. The lionesses are the hunters. They give birth to about three or four cubs every two years. The mother feeds the cubs and teaches them to hunt. After about three years, the older male lions cast out the younger ones. Sometimes, though, the young males drive away their male elders.

Speedy Fact 1

A lion's roar can be heard for 5 miles (8 km).

Speedy Fact 2

When lions sleep, they hold their tails straight out, not curled around their bodies like house cats.

Speedy Fact 3

Lions sleep in dens or rest under trees most of the day. They usually hunt at night.

Speedy Fact 4

When a lion is threatened, it pulls back its lips and twitches the tuft of black hair at the end of its tail.

Fearsome Teeth

Lions are like all hunting animals. They have long, sharp canine teeth in the front of their mouths. These teeth grab, stab, tear, and hold on to prey as the prey struggles. Lions' molar teeth have sharp ridges for cutting up meat.

Lionesses hunt in groups of three or four. When they find a herd of zebras, antelopes, or wild pigs, the lionesses form a circle around the prey and hide, crouched down in the tall grass. Suddenly, one lioness stands up. This frightens the prey and it flees—right toward the other lionesses. Working together, the lionesses separate a slower or weaker animal from the herd. With a rush, a lioness leaps on the victim. She sinks her teeth into its neck. The hunt is over.

Speedy Fact 1

Because they work together, lionesses can kill animals bigger than themselves.

Speedy Fact 2

After a hunt, a lioness drags her victim, which can weigh 250 pounds (113.4 kg), to a shady spot, sometimes up in a tree. This keeps the prey safe from other animals.

Speedy Fact 3

Male lions eat first, lionesses second, and finally the cubs—if there is meat left on the bones.

DOGS
The Family Way

In many ways, a dog behaves much like its wild ancestor, the wolf. A female dog looks for a dark, warm place to give birth. That is like the female wolf going into an underground den to bear her pups. Dogs turn around several times before lying down. This is similar to wolves walking in small circles to flatten grass for their bed.

Dogs often bury bones. This inborn behavior comes from the way wolves bury meat left over after killing a very large animal. Wolves dig up the meat and eat it later. Most dogs gobble their food like wolves. This behavior probably springs from an inborn fear that other animals will grab it. The expression "wolf down food," which means to "eat fast," comes from this behavior.

Speedy Fact 1
A weaker dog—or wolf— holds its tail between its legs. The stronger dog holds its tail high in the air to show its higher standing.

Speedy Fact 2
To show it wants to play, a dog lowers the front part of its body while keeping the back part up in the air.

Speedy Fact 3
A dog can drink muddy water or eat rotten meat and not get sick. Chemicals in a dog's stomach kill the germs.

Speedy Fact 4
Dogs urinate on trees, rocks, or posts to let other dogs know that they have been there.

Speedy Fact 5
When excited, some dogs stand on their hind feet and punch with their front paws.

Quick and Sharp

Dogs mostly use their eyes, ears, and sense of smell to find food and avoid danger. To pick up faint smells, they hold their noses close to the ground or to the objects they are smelling. A dog's sense of smell is a million times better than a human's sense of smell. Dogs turn their large, erect ears to pick up sounds and locate their direction.

More than many other animals, dogs have the ability to learn commands and do different jobs. Some even seem able to use their intelligence to solve problems—including bringing newspapers. In one experiment, dogs learned how to get food rewards by pressing a button.

Speedy Fact 1
A dog can tell whether another dog is a friend or enemy by smelling the gland just under its tail.

Speedy Fact 2
Bloodhounds can follow a scent trail that is ten days old.

Speedy Fact 3
Shepherd dogs in Switzerland are able to smell people buried under 20 feet (6 m) of snow.

Speedy Fact 4
Dogs lick their noses to keep them wet. A wet nose helps a dog pick up smells.

Speedy Fact 5
When a dog gets too hot, it sticks out its tongue and pants. The extra air cools off its body.

13

Helping People

Today there are many ways that dogs help people. Some dogs are trained to "see" for people who are blind or "hear" for people who are deaf. Other dogs learn to help those who can't use parts of their body, or to be friends with the old, sick, or lonely. Working dogs also herd sheep, guard people or places, catch criminals, pull sleds, and sniff for drugs or explosives.

Some helping-dog behaviors come from dogs' wolf ancestors. A pointer points its nose at hidden animals to help hunters find their prey. The leader of a wolf pack also stops and points in the direction of the prey it smells.

Speedy Fact 1

A guide dog, or Seeing Eye dog, knows about 20 different commands. A guide dog cannot see colors, but it can tell when a traffic light changes from red to green.

Speedy Fact 2

A hearing dog nudges a deaf person awake when the alarm clock rings. The dog also alerts someone to a ringing phone or a knock on the door.

Speedy Fact 3

An assistance dog can find and bring things to someone confined to bed. They can also open and close doors and turn the TV and radio on and off.

Speedy Fact 4

Gary Wimer spent 20 minutes a day teaching a golden retriever to add, subtract, multiply, and divide. The dog barked the correct answers.

Rescue Animals

Rescue dogs show great bravery, loyalty, and intelligence in times of crisis. Many even give their own lives to save or protect their human masters.

Perhaps the most famous rescue dog is Balto, an Alaskan husky. In January 1925, several children in Nome, Alaska, were very sick. There was neither medicine in Nome to treat them nor any roads or railways to Nome. Balto led a dog team that carried the much-needed medicine to the Alaskan city. Doctors said that the medicine saved hundreds of lives. People later erected a statue to Balto's memory in New York's Central Park.

Speedy Fact 1

On September 11, 2001, Salty, a guide dog, led his owner to safety down 71 flights of stairs after the World Trade Center attack.

Speedy Fact 2

In 1800, a St. Bernard named Barry found and rescued 40 people who had been lost in the Swiss Alps.

Speedy Fact 3

During World War 1, named Stubby caught held a German spy, s the lives of many Ameri soldiers. Stubby grabbed the spy because unfamili

Speedy Fact 4

In 1972, Brandy, a German shepherd, investigated a bomb threat in an airplane. She found the bomb—exactly 12 minutes before it was set to go off!

HORSES
Horse Sense

Imagine you are face-to-face with a horse. The first things you see are the horse's long head and large, egg-shaped eyes. The eyes keep the horse safe. They let the horse view a wide area. They also allow the horse to eat grass and look out for enemies at the same time.

A long face and large nose give the horse a very good sense of smell, too. The horse's short, pointed, upright ears are like an early-warning system. A horse can turn its ears to receive sounds from almost any direction. A horse's ears also let others know the horse's mood. An angry horse twitches its ears or lays them back against its head. A horse that has one ear facing forward and one backward is confused by what is going on.

Speedy Fact 1

Horses have a very good sense of touch. They twitch special muscles to get rid of flies and other annoying insects.

Speedy Fact 2

A horse's eyes adjust slowly to changes of light. A horse often gets fidgety until it can see clearly.

Speedy Fact 3

Strong winds or heavy rain interfere with a horse's good sense of smell. This explains why horses often get nervous in bad weather.

Alert and Brainy

Horses are highly intelligent animals. They can be trained to ride, race, jump, hunt, play polo, pull wagons, and stand on their rear legs. Horses seem to have excellent memories and can remember pleasant or unpleasant experiences for many years.

Horses are also very good at following commands. Riders can give orders by voice, by hand, by leg, or by reins. Horses are usually very willing to follow instructions. Most horses easily overcome their fear of strange riders, new places, and unfamiliar situations.

Speedy Fact 1

Race horses learn to run faster when they feel a touch from their jockey's whip.

Speedy Fact 2

Horses may suddenly rear up and bolt when faced with an object or place that brings back a bad memory.

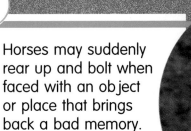

Speedy Fact 3

Horses often break out of their stalls just before an earthquake occurs. The animals seem to sense an approaching disaster.

Speedy Fact 4

Horses roll over on the ground to relax their muscles. This behavior also gets rid of loose hairs, dirt, and any bugs in their coats.

17

ELEPHANTS
Huge and Hefty

Elephants are big in every way. Besides being the largest land animals, elephants eat and drink more than any other land animal. An adult elephant eats about 330 pounds (150 kg) of food and drinks 40 gallons (150 l) of water every day. Elephants in the wild spend as many as 16 hours daily eating and drinking.

Inside an elephant's big head is a huge brain. People train elephants to do circus tricks, such as marching around in a circle, rising up on their rear legs, and even standing on their head. Humans have also taught working elephants to haul logs and pull wagons.

Speedy Fact 1
A charging elephant can run 25 miles per hour (40 kph) for a short distance. But elephants can't jump.

Speedy Fact 2
When an elephant raises its trunk and calls, the sound can be heard for 6 miles (9.7 km). Elephants call to meet, greet, or warn others of danger.

Speedy Fact 3
Elephants can knock over or pull up small trees. This allows them to reach the tender leaves that grow at the top.

Speedy Fact 4
Working elephants obey as many as 40 different voice commands. The elephant learns to carry tourists and lift heavy objects, among other tasks.

Elephants make about 25 different low, rumbling calls, each with a different meaning.

Elephant Herds

Wild elephants live in herds of 10 to 50. The leader is usually a large, older female elephant. The herd stays together to make it easier to find food and water and to protect the sick and young. Elephants use screams, roars, bellows, groans, and squeaks to communicate.

The elephants in a herd take care of one another. Sometimes they also take care of elephants from different herds. Years ago, two moviemakers filming elephants at a watering hole startled the herd. The animals fled, accidentally leaving one small calf behind. Several hyenas appeared, ready to attack the calf. Suddenly a second herd of elephants arrived. They drove the hyenas away. The calf was last seen walking with the new herd.

Speedy Fact
2

Female elephants in a herd, called "aunts," help a mother elephant care for her newborn calf.

Speedy Fact
3

A scared calf makes a coarse, loud rumble. The mother elephant calms her baby with a soft, humming rumble and strokes it with her trunk.

Speedy Fact
4

When a tiger or other animal attacks, the elephant herd forms a circle around the calves to protect them.

Speedy Fact
5

Two elephants say "hello" by placing the tips of their trunks in each other's mouth.

BEARS
Hungry and Short-tempered

Most bears in the wild eat almost anything—and are always hungry. Grizzly bears feed on all foods, from small animals and fish to grass and roots. Polar bears like to catch seals and walruses. Sun bears prefer honey. Termites and ants are favorite meals for sloth bears. But panda bears are very fussy—they eat only bamboo.

Bears are usually peaceful. They try to run away from fights and from danger. But they do have bad tempers and get angry very easily. Bears attack anyone who seems to threaten them, their cubs, or their food.

Speedy Fact 1
Bears dig up roots, gather fruit and berries, and break open beehives with their claws.

Speedy Fact 2
When a grizzly bear catches a fish, the bear strips off all the flesh, leaving nothing but the head, bones, and tail.

Speedy Fact 3
A sloth bear breaks open termite nests with its claws, sticks its snout into the smashed nest, and loudly slurps up the termites.

Speedy Fact 4
The Malayan sun bear hooks its claws into bark to help it climb trees.

Sleeping Through Winter

A bear sleeps very deeply through the coldest months. While asleep, it does not eat or drink. It lives off the fat stored in its body. Its heartbeat slows and its temperature drops.

Some say that the bear hibernates (HYE-bur-nates). But most scientists now agree that it is not a true hibernation. The bear just goes into a deep winter sleep. Its temperature and heart rate do not drop as far as those of true hibernating animals. And it does not sleep as soundly as the hibernators. A loud noise or another animal will rouse a sleeping bear. On warm days the bear may wake up by itself, go for a stroll, and then return to sleep.

ANTS
Down to Earth

Ants are the most common insects on earth. You find them in almost every part of the world. Like some humans, ants live and work in large, citylike communities, called *colonies*. A colony can have hundreds or even thousands of ants sharing a single nest in the ground.

Most of the ants in a colony are workers. But not all workers have the same job. Some dig out tunnels in the soil to build the nest. Others guard the nest and keep it clean. Still others gather food and bring it back to the nest. A few feed and care for the young. Only one ant in the colony, the queen, lays the eggs from which all the ants are born.

Speedy Fact 2

Leaf-cutter ants carry bits of leaves back to their nest and chew them into mush. The mush sprouts mush-roomlike growths that the ants eat.

Speedy Fact 1

A worker ant that guards the nest may shove its head into the entrance to stop others from entering.

Speedy Fact 5

An ant can tell a nestmate from a stranger by its smell. Ants often fight strangers but share food and touch antennae with nestmates.

Speedy Fact 3

In winter, ants hibernate in the deepest rooms inside their nests.

Speedy Fact 4

Army ants march through the jungle in huge troops, with millions of members.

1

Ants rub their bodies on the ground as they hunt for food. This leaves an odor trail for other ants to follow.

Eating In

The food that an ant eats depends on where and how it lives. Harvester ants live in dry, sandy areas. They eat seeds of grains and wild grasses. Honey ants live among flowers and fill themselves with honey. Army ants mostly eat tiny insects.

Some honey ants swell up like little balls from eating lots of honey. These ants hang themselves on walls of the nest. To get honey, other ants tap the honey ants with their feelers. This makes the hanging ants spit up some honey for the others to eat. So-called slave ants feed Amazon ants that cannot feed themselves.

2

Harvester ants make "ant bread" by chewing the seeds they collect. The ants eat the bread when food is scarce.

3

Ants carry loads that are about 50 times their own weight. If you were that strong, you could lift a 2-ton (2.1-t) truck!

4

Certain kinds of ants attack and eat caterpillars. This helps save the trees, since caterpillars, which are the larvae of moths and butterflies, are huge eaters of leaves.

KANGAROOS
Get Up and Go

Kangaroos know how to get around. They cannot walk like other two-legged or four-legged animals. But they sure are able to hop fast.

Kangaroos are grazing animals. They spend almost all their time eating grass, as well as a few plants and shrubs. Water is scarce in Australia, where most kangaroos live. Kangaroos get much of the liquid they need from eating grass. Kangaroos can go for weeks, or even months, without drinking a drop of water.

Speedy Fact 1

Kangaroos sometimes gather at feeding sites in large herds, or "mobs."

Speedy Fact 2

Kangaroos throw dust into the air to protect themselves from flies and other insects.

Speedy Fact 3

Kangaroos pant like dogs to cool off. When overheated, they sometimes scoop away the topsoil and rest on the cooler layer below.

Speedy Fact 4

Mob members look out for danger. They loudly stamp their strong hind feet to warn of danger.

Speedy Fact 5

Kangaroo toes also work as "combs" to smooth fur and scratch behind their ears.

LENGTH OF JUMPS

Animal	feet	meters
Frog	10	3
Rabbit	10	3
Human	29.5	8.9
Kangaroo	30	9

feet	5	10	15	20	25	3
meters	1.5	3	4.5	6	7.5	

Bringing Up Joey

A young kangaroo is called a joey. A joey is born tiny, hairless, and blind. With all of its strength, a joey climbs up through the fur of its mother's belly and into her pocket-shaped pouch. The joey's journey has been compared to a human baby using only its arms to crawl 10 feet (3 m) up a steep hill with eyes closed to reach its mother's lap!

The newborn joey drinks its mother's milk. At about nine months of age, the joey is ready to leave the pouch for short periods. The young kangaroo gradually spends less and less time inside the pouch and finally moves out altogether.

Speedy Fact 1

A kangaroo mother grooms her joey and licks dust from its head. She often makes soft, sucking noises at the same time.

Speedy Fact 2

A frightened joey on the ground will jump back into the pouch headfirst. The joey then turns itself over and sticks out its head.

Speedy Fact 3

A mother warns her joey with a quick, loud stamp of a hind foot. This also acts as an alarm for the rest of the mob.

Speedy Fact 4

Young male kangaroos often wrestle with their mothers. This play fighting helps the joey build muscles and learn to fend for itself.

RABBITS
Home Life

Most rabbits live in shallow holes, called *forms*. Rabbits dig forms in meadows or fields, usually in places well-hidden by shrubs or tall grass. Other rabbits make their home inside underground tunnels, called *warrens*. Rabbits also live in burrows that may have once been home to families of skunks, woodchucks, or prairie dogs.

A female rabbit generally gives birth to four or five babies, called *kits*, at a time. To keep the young warm, the mother covers them with grass and with fur that she pulls off her chest with her teeth. The mother feeds the kits milk for about two weeks after birth. By the time they are six months old they can have babies of their own.

Fact

1 Rabbits hop. They cannot walk or run like most other four-legged animals.

2 A rabbit uses its long, strong hind legs for leaping and its shorter front legs to keep steady. This is like balancing on your hands while playing leapfrog.

Speedy Fact

4 A mother rabbit does not stay in the nest with her kits, but she remains nearby.

A rabbit seems to twitch its nose almost all the time. A good sense of smell alerts it to danger.

Staying Alive

Like many small animals, rabbits must avoid becoming prey to foxes, wolves, and other enemies. Rabbits cannot use their teeth or claws to fight off attackers. But they do have ways of protecting themselves. Eyes on either side of their head give rabbits a wide field of vision. Also, rabbits can move their long ears, either together or separately, to catch the softest sounds of a nearby enemy.

When threatened, a rabbit hides or remains very still in the hope it will not be seen. To escape, a rabbit hops away at high speed. One leap can carry a rabbit more than 10 feet (3 m).

Speedy Fact 1

An older male often acts as a lookout for a group of rabbits. If frightened, he thumps loudly with his hind legs.

Speedy Fact 2

Most rabbits look for food at night and rest during the day.

Speedy Fact 3

Most rabbits scream when caught in a trap. Foot thumps and screams are the only two sounds they make.

Speedy Fact 4

Rabbits and dogs can play together. Sometimes they can be seen chasing each other or cuddling.

Speedy Fact 5

Rabbits rarely travel farther than a quarter mile (0.4 km) from their birthplace. If chased by a fox, a rabbit will run to the border and change direction, but not cross the invisible line.

ANIMALS IN THE TREES
MONKEYS
Life in the Trees

Most monkeys live in tropical forests and spend their time running, jumping, and swinging from high tree branches. Only a few larger monkeys, such as baboons, live mostly on the ground. Tree-dwellers usually have longer back legs and longer tails than ground-dwelling monkeys.

All monkeys belong to groups, which range from just a few members to hundreds. Being part of a group helps the monkeys find food and avoid their enemies. The groups stay together by sound, such as the howls of howler monkeys, the whoops of Asian leaf monkeys, and the roars of colobus monkeys.

Speedy Fact 1

A monkey's tail is like a fifth hand. The animal wraps its tail around branches and uses it to grasp fruit and other objects.

Speedy Fact 2

Squirrel monkeys scamper through the trees like their namesakes.

Speedy Fact 4

Titi monkeys live together in groups. They twist their tails together when they go to sleep.

Speedy Fact 3

The howler monkey is among the loudest of all animals. Its screams, which can be heard for 3 miles (5 km) in the jungle, help it keep in touch with others in its group and mark its territory.

Monkey Helpers

Capuchin (KAP-yoo-shin) monkeys are the most intelligent of all monkeys. In the wild, they live in groups as large as 40 monkeys. Often, an entire group will swoop down on a farm, scatter, and start stealing fruit from the trees. With so many monkeys, the farmer doesn't stand a chance of shooing them all away.

Capuchins make good helpers for people. Trainers have taught capuchins to help people who are unable to move their arms or legs. The monkeys can turn the pages in a book, feed their owner, open bottles, and even scratch a person's itch. It takes about six years of training to prepare a capuchin to become an assistance pet.

Speedy Fact 1
To crack the hard shells of the palm nuts they eat, capuchins hold on to a branch with their tails and slam the nuts against another branch.

Speedy Fact 2
A capuchin monkey can break off a tree branch and use it as a tool to pull food closer.

Speedy Fact 3
Capuchins rub a spicy pepper plant on their fur to rid themselves of insects.

Speedy Fact 4
Sometimes capuchins come down from trees to hunt for crabs and clams in jungle swamps.

Speedy Fact 5
Capuchins can run on their two rear legs while holding something in their hands.

29

CHIMPANZEES
Top Banana

Chimpanzees are apes that make their home in the rain forest. The chimps roam far and wide, in trees and on the ground, looking for food. They spend much of each day searching for the ripe fruit, leaves, seeds, and insects that they eat. When moving on the ground, a chimpanzee walks on all fours, supporting its upper body on the knuckles of its hands.

Chimpanzees either travel in small groups or alone. At night, chimpanzees sleep in high, leafy tree nests that they make up fresh each night. Adults sleep alone, except when they have infants to care for. Baby chimpanzees sleep with their mothers.

Speedy Fact 1

To show off their strength, male chimpanzees sometimes walk upright, waving branches and screaming.

Speedy Fact 2

A young chimp stays with its mother for about five years. At first, it rides under the mother's body, holding on to her furry belly. Later, it rides on her back.

Speedy Fact 3

Young chimps like to play. They chase one another, wrestle, climb, and swing from trees.

Speedy Fact 4

Adult chimps spend about an hour a day grooming—removing dirt, insects, leaves, or burrs from one another's long, black hair.

Speedy Fact 5

Chimps are good climbers. Their big toes are like thumbs that can grasp branches while climbing.

Noisy and Clever

Chimpanzees bark, grunt, and scream to keep in touch with others in the rain forest. They also use body posture and facial expressions to show their moods and feelings.

Chimpanzees are the most intelligent apes and among the smartest of all animals. In the wild, chimps make simple tools of tree branches to stick in termite nests and pull out the termites. They also use stones as weapons or to crack nuts. When they're thirsty, chimps mash up some leaves, dip them in water, and squeeze the water into their mouths. In zoos, chimpanzees pile up boxes to reach fruit that is beyond their grasp. Thanks to an excellent memory, chimps can be trained to perform tricks in shows or movies. Most amazing of all, chimps can learn to communicate with humans by hand signals!

Speedy Fact 1

A chimpanzee jumps up and down, hoots loudly, and beats on tree trunks to call others when it finds a large food supply.

Speedy Fact 2

A young chimp learns by imitating adults. It watches its mother bend tree branches to make a nest and then the young chimp practices the task until it can do it well.

Speedy Fact 3

In four years Washoe, a female chimp, learned 130 words in sign language. The first time she saw a swan, she signed "water bird."

Speedy Fact 4

During the 1970s and 1980s, a chimpanzee named Lana learned to use a computer keyboard to ask for food, music, or someone to stay with her.

Speedy Fact 5

A chimpanzee signals great fear or excitement by pulling back its lips and showing its gums and teeth. Take care not to mistake the look for a smile!

31

GORILLAS
Big and Fierce-looking

Gorillas in real life are very different from the gorillas you see in movies. Big, powerful, and fierce-looking, gorillas are actually slow-moving, peaceful animals that tend to be shy and friendly. Gorillas will not attack a person unless they are annoyed or threatened.

The gorilla makes its home in the rain forests of central Africa. Small groups of gorillas travel through the forests with an adult male always in the lead. The gorillas look for their food—fruits, leaves, roots, and bark—in the forest. The gorillas usually move along the ground, but may climb into trees to sit or eat.

Speedy Fact **1**
An excited gorilla stands up on its legs and slaps its cupped hands against its chest. The loud, drumlike sound seems to frighten away other animals and humans.

Speedy Fact **2**
Gorillas stand or sit upright to eat. This leaves their hands free to hold food.

Speedy Fact **3**
When angry, a male gorilla may let out a loud roar.

Speedy Fact **4**
Gorillas sometimes seem to be yawning. This look usually signals fright, not sleepiness.

Speedy Fact **5**
Gorillas often end their meals with loud burps.

Call It a Day

A gorilla's day begins at dawn. The head male gorilla leads the group to its first feeding place. Here, the gorillas chomp down their food for about two hours. From mid-morning to mid-afternoon, the group rests. Adult gorillas either nap or groom one another; the young play and swing from the trees.

After resting, it's time to travel on and find the next feeding place. Here, the gorillas eat until dusk, when the group builds nests of branches in the trees or on the ground. They sleep for about 12 hours. The group awakens at dawn and sets off on another day of wandering in the forest.

ANIMALS IN THE AIR
PARROTS
Birds of a Feather

Parrots are found in warm, tropical countries all around the world. They are noisy, social birds that flock together in large groups. Parrots are fast flyers and they travel long distances looking for food. There are more than 300 different kinds of parrots, and most spend their lives in trees, eating, climbing, and squawking at one another.

Lovebirds are a kind of small parrot. The name comes from the way the birds pair off into male-female couples that snuggle and rub each other with their bills. In the wild, lovebirds carry grass and straw under their feathers to line their nests. Captive lovebirds often make nest linings out of strips of paper that they tear and tuck beneath their feathers.

1 The kea parrot of New Zealand often begs for food.

2 Like bats, hanging parrots sleep dangling upside down from tree branches.

3 Parrots hold food or other objects with their feet. They always scratch their heads with the same foot.

4 To see forward, a parrot must turn its head. That's because a parrot's eyes are on the sides of its head.

Smart Bird Brains

"Bird brain" usually means "not very smart." But this does not apply to parrots, which are very intelligent. Parrots can learn to imitate, or mimic, human speech. Some experts say parrots can think as well as just copy sounds.

A scientist named Irene Pepperberg spent 20 years teaching Alex, an African gray parrot, to say about 100 different words. Alex also learned to identify 7 colors and 5 shapes, and could count to 6. One time, Alex got sick and Dr. Pepperberg had to leave him at the vet's office. As she headed for the door, Alex called out, "Come here. I love you. I want to go back."

Speedy Fact 1

Small parrots, called parakeets, are natural acrobats. They can do many tricks on ladders and swings.

Speedy Fact 2

Parrots sometimes sense when an earthquake is coming. People reported that some birds started to screech about fifteen minutes before the San Francisco earthquake of 1989.

Speedy Fact 3

Parrots stretch their necks and hiss when angry.

Speedy Fact 4

Parrots strut and flare their feathers to show off.

PIGEONS
City Birds

Have you ever wondered why you usually see pigeons in the city and not in the country? Scientists believe it is because pigeons find more food in cities than they find elsewhere—even though their favorite foods are grains and seeds.

In the city, pigeons can nest on narrow ledges, spaces between buildings, and hidden roof corners. This is not very different from the behavior of pigeons and their cousins, the doves, in the wild. They often build nests on or around high, rocky cliffs. Finally, pigeons seem to have fewer natural enemies in cities than they do in the wild.

Speedy Fact 1
Most city pigeons get food from people or garbage. Their drinking water comes from puddles or fountains.

Speedy Fact 2
Pigeons waterproof their feathers with powder from special feathers called powderdowns.

Speedy Fact 3
When flying, a pigeon's wings strike each other above the pigeon's back. This makes a clapping noise.

Speedy Fact 4
Pigeon feathers come out more easily than feathers of most other birds. So when a cat leaps on a pigeon, it gets a mouthful of feathers and the bird can escape.

Speedy Fact 5
A female pigeon only lays eggs in the presence of other pigeons. Scientists sometimes put a mirror in the nest to fool the bird.

In ancient Greece, homing pigeons brought news of the Olympic games to distant cities.

During World War I, a homing pigeon named Cher Ami flew about 24 miles (39 km) to deliver a message, even though one leg had been shot off and it had a bullet wound in its chest.

Trainers know that a homing pigeon will surely return if it leaves a young pigeon in its nest.

Roller and tumbler pigeons flip over backward as they fly.

Unusual Ways

Pigeons differ from other birds in a few ways. Most birds tip their head back to swallow water. But a pigeon uses its beak like a straw to suck up water without raising its head. Most male and female birds change partners from year to year. Pigeons seem to stay together for life. Many birds sleep with their heads tucked under one of their wings. Pigeons pull their heads in close to their bodies.

Many birds find their way over long distances. But certain kinds of pigeons, called homing pigeons, can return home from as far as 1,000 miles (1,600 km) away. People train some of these pigeons to race at great speeds as well as carry messages to and from a destination.

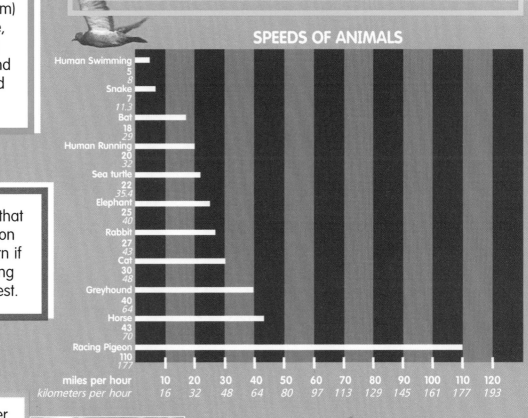

SPEEDS OF ANIMALS

Animal	mph	km/h
Human Swimming	5	8
Snake	7	11.3
Bat	18	29
Human Running	20	32
Sea turtle	22	35.4
Elephant	25	40
Rabbit	27	43
Cat	30	48
Greyhound	40	64
Horse	43	70
Racing Pigeon	110	177

miles per hour	10	20	30	40	50	60	70	80	90	100	110	120
kilometers per hour	16	32	48	64	80	97	113	129	145	161	177	193

BATS
Strange Creatures

Bats fly with their hands, see with their ears, and sleep hanging by the toes of their hind feet!

Bats' wings are made of a thin skin that covers the finger bones of their hands. Most bats fly in the dark of night. They make about 50 squeaks a second as they fly. The sounds are so high-pitched that humans cannot hear them. Bats find their way by listening for the echoes of these sounds. This is called *echolocation*. If the sound bounces back quickly, the bats know that something—a bug, bird, tree, or wall—is nearby. Echoes that take a long time to return tell the bats that the animal or object is farther away. When bats go to sleep, they lock their toes around a perch and hang upside down without falling.

Speedy Fact 1
Using echolocation, a bat can fly between wires 12 inches (30.5 cm) apart without hitting them.

Speedy Fact 2
Fruit-eating bats drop seeds from their mouths. Some of these seeds grow into new plants.

Speedy Fact 3
Fishing bats fly low over rivers and lakes and grab small fish near the surface with their sharp claws.

Speedy Fact 4
Meat-eating bats swoop down and grab frogs or mice with their long, sharp teeth.

Speedy Fact 5
Vampire bats make a tiny cut in the skin of a sleeping cow or horse, lap up the blood, and fly away before the animal wakes.

In the Dark

Most bats hunt only at night. That is when the moths and mosquitoes they like to eat are flying around. Also, many of the flowers that bats feed on open only after dark. And many of the bats' enemies are fast asleep.

During the day, most bats sleep in caves, barns, attics, or hollow trees. The largest bat colony is in Bracken Cave in Texas. As many as 20 million bats roost there every day. In the summer, some of the females at Bracken Cave give birth to tiny babies called pups. There are so many pups that they hang down over all the walls and ceilings of the cave.

Speedy Fact 1

In one night, a gray bat can catch—and swallow—as many as 3,000 insects.

Speedy Fact 2

Bat pups huddle together to keep warm.

Speedy Fact 3

Each mother bat can find its pup by scent alone.

Speedy Fact 4

When the mother finds its pup, she washes its face with her tongue and feeds it milk from her body.

Speedy Fact 5

Only in time of danger does the mother carry her pup to a new home.

WATER/LAND ANIMALS
FROGS
A Double Life

Tadpoles

Frogs spend part of their life in water and part on land. Some kinds of frogs spend their entire lives in or near water. Others live mainly on land but come to water to mate and lay eggs.

Female frogs lay anywhere from 1,000 to 3,000 eggs at a time. Most then leave. But certain frogs have special ways to protect their eggs. Female brooding frogs hold the eggs inside their stomachs until they hatch into tadpoles, which swim out through the mother's open mouth. Male midwife toads, which are really frogs, wrap a string of eggs around their hind legs and walk around with them for about a month. They then drop the eggs into a pond or stream where the eggs hatch.

Speedy Fact 1

Frogs shoot out their long tongues to catch the insects they like to eat. The insects get caught on the sticky tip.

Speedy Fact 2

Frogs rarely drink water. Certain ones sit down in damp or wet places and water comes in through their bottoms.

Speedy Fact 3

Frogs blink their eyes when they eat. This pushes their eyeballs down on top of their mouths and helps squeeze the food down.

Speedy Fact 4

Frogs are fussy eaters. If they eat something they don't like, they throw up their entire stomachs. After the bad food has fallen out, the frog swallows its stomach again.

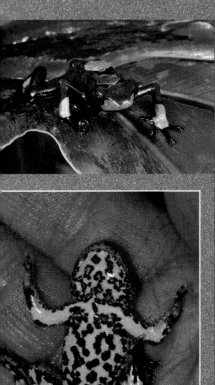

Escape Artists

Frogs have many enemies, such as snakes, birds, rats, foxes, and fish. Frogs have a few ways to escape harm. Some blend in with the ground and plants and are hard to find. Others simply flee, leaping with long, powerful hind legs to get away. Often, frogs jump into a pond or stream and use the webbed toes on their hind feet to swim away— and fast!

A poisonous skin protects many frogs. These frogs taste awful and their poison can kill an enemy. Poisonous frogs are often bright red, green, or yellow. Once an attacking animal tastes one of these frogs, it knows to stay away from them.

Speedy Fact 1
When in danger, the yellow-belly toad turns its rear legs over, showing a bright orange patch with blue spots. This scares away most foes.

Speedy Fact 2
South American bullfrogs make a foam nest in the water to protect their eggs and then the tadpoles from enemies.

Speedy Fact 3
Moving backward, frogs dig into piles of dead leaves. The leaves hide the frog and keep its skin moist as it waits for an unlucky insect to come along.

Speedy Fact 4
When frogs leap to escape an attacker, they close their eyes for protection.

41

TURTLES
Keeping Safe

Turtles walk around with their houses on their backs. Their shells cover both the top and bottom of their bodies. The shells are like a suit of armor that protects the turtle. The turtle's head and legs stick out of the shells. But it quickly tucks its head and legs into its shells when there is danger. Some turtles, such as box turtles, can snap the two shells together, keeping their whole bodies safe inside.

Certain turtles spend all their time in freshwater ponds and streams. You find different kinds only on land. A number can survive on land or in water. Sea turtles swim in the world's oceans.

Speedy Fact 1
Turtles spend most of their time basking in the sun to get warm. When they are too hot, they either seek a shady spot or dive into water.

Speedy Fact 3
Stinkpots give off an awful smell to ward off enemies.

Speedy Fact 2
Snapping turtles bite enemies with their sharp, powerful beaks.

Speedy Fact 5
In places with severe winters, turtles hibernate. They sleep through the cold months hidden in the soil or water.

Speedy Fact 4
An African pancake turtle hides inside a crack in a rock. It puffs up its body so that it can't be pulled out.

Toothless Wonders

A turtle has no teeth. It catches and cuts its food with its sharp, powerful beak. If a turtle catches a fish or animal too big to swallow, it can easily cut it in half with just one bite.

Turtles can't run and are slow walkers. But they can whip their head out with amazing speed to nab nearby food. For example, the African helmeted turtle eats birds. The turtle sits at the edge of a pond. When a small bird hops over for a drink, the turtle shoots out its head and snatches the unlucky creature in its beak.

Speedy Fact 1

The alligator snapping turtle wiggles the red tip of its tongue in the water. As soon as a fish goes for this bait, the turtle snaps its jaws shut.

Speedy Fact 2

The matamata turtle waits for fish on a river bottom. When its prey comes near, the turtle opens its throat wide and sucks the fish into its mouth.

Speedy Fact 3

The Australian snake-necked turtle wraps its long neck around its sides until it's time to catch fish. Then watch out!

Speedy Fact 4

Some turtles will eat anything that is red. Zookeepers hide medicines for these turtles in tomatoes!

SNAKES
On the Move

Snakes have no legs and slide along on their bellies. But how do they move? On the ground, most snakes form their bodies into S-shaped curves. Then they push the back part of each curve against a bump, rock, or plant on the ground. This propels them forward. Snakes that live in the water swim by forming S curves and pushing against the water.

Some snakes climb trees. They press against the tree so that their scaly bodies grab on to the bark. Viper snakes can jump. They coil their bodies like springs and shoot straight up. Snakes cannot fly, but some flatten their bodies and glide down from high tree branches.

Speedy Fact

1

Viper snakes hide among long, green vines. Enemies have a hard time finding them.

Speedy Fact

2

Some tree snakes grab branches with their tails and hang down.

Speedy Fact

3

So-called "flying snakes" can glide down as far as 80 feet (24 m) from branch to branch.

Speedy Fact

4

A pipe snake uses its head to wiggle through the damp soil or mud in the rice fields and swamps where it lives. When attacked, it hides its head and waves its tail.

Poison Power

About 20 percent of all kinds of snakes are poisonous. The poison gives a snake some great advantages. Certain poisons kill prey. Others quiet prey so that it doesn't fight back and injure the snake.

The snake stores the poison in glands on each side of its upper jaw. When attacking, the snake squeezes the poison into long, hollow teeth, called fangs. Then it bites. The fangs inject poison into the unlucky victim.

1

Snakes bite people only when annoyed. A bite can take less than a quarter of a second.

Speedy Fact 2

The rattlesnake is poisonous. But it does not shake its rattles when it is ready to bite.

Every year, 1,000 people in the United States are bitten by rattlesnakes. Of these people, 980 survive and 20 die.

20 people, or 2%, die.

980 people, or 98%, survive.

Speedy Fact 3

Three kinds of cobras spit poison at an attacker's eyes. The poison burns and can cause blindness.

Speedy Fact 4

King cobra snakes sometimes bite elephants. An elephant nipped by a king cobra will die within four hours.

45

CROCODILES
Fake Tears

Long ago, people believed that crocodiles shed fake tears as they ate their victims. "Crocodile tears" came to mean false sadness. Today we know that crocodiles are large, powerful animals that feed on many different animals—but they don't cry. The crocodile diet ranges from small insects, fish, and birds, to large lions, tigers, and antelopes.

Crocodiles live in the shallow water of swamps, marshes, and slow-flowing rivers. In water, they sweep their tails from side to side to swim at high speeds. On land, the crocodile usually crawls along the ground on its belly. When running, the animal lifts up its body. Crocodiles' webbed feet let them move fast on muddy, soft ground.

Speedy Fact 1

Most crocodiles eat once a week. This is far fewer than the 21 meals a week you eat.

Speedy Fact 2

Crocodiles grab animals that come to the water to drink, pull them into the water, and hold the creatures down until they drown.

Speedy Fact 3

Crocodiles can run quickly but can't change direction easily. To escape a crocodile, run in a zigzag path.

Speedy Fact 4

Giant crocodiles let little plover birds enter their mouths and pick out leftover bits of food. The crocodiles get clean teeth while the birds have a tasty dinner.

Labor of Love

Before they mate, male and female crocodiles rub their snouts together, swim around in circles, and blow bubbles in the water. They also "talk" to each other in growls, coughs, and purrs.

Female crocodiles build nests on land but near water. Some just dig a hole in the sand or soil. Others make a pile of rotting plants, twigs, and grass. The mother lays 20 to 60 eggs and buries them in the nest. As the eggs start to hatch, the babies grunt and chirp and the mother digs them out. If there is any danger, the mother takes the babies into her mouth and carries them to a safe place.

Speedy Fact 1

A female crocodile guards the nest for the three months until the eggs hatch.

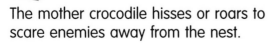

Speedy Fact 2

The mother crocodile hisses or roars to scare enemies away from the nest.

Speedy Fact 3

A mother crocodile often carries her young in her mouth or on her back. This protects the baby from predators.

ANIMAL WAYS

Life in the wild for most animals is very difficult. There is a daily struggle to find food and avoid enemies. Some animals must find ways to cool off in very hot weather. Others need to be able to keep warm in freezing cold. All animals need to bear young and keep in touch with others of their own kind.

In this book, you have read about some of the many behaviors that help animals survive. Lions use their size, power, and sharp teeth to catch other animals. Some snakes kill their victims by biting them with poisonous fangs. Bears smash open beehives for the honey.

Small animals have ways of acting that protect them from enemy attacks. Rabbits stay absolutely still to avoid being seen. Frogs leap away at high speed. Monkeys screech or squawk loudly.

Almost all animals have very keen senses that tell them about their surroundings. Bats find their way by making sounds and listening for the echoes. Cats can see in the dark. Dogs have a sense of smell a million times better than humans.

Animals' different behaviors help them survive in their environment. As the environment changes over thousands of years, the animals change. These changes go on forever. They are part of the endless struggle of life on Earth.